ANIMAL BABIES

I0804265

BABY COWS

by Jennifer Boothroyd

Consultant: Beth Gambro
Reading Specialist, Yorkville, Illinois

BEARPORT PUBLISHING

Minneapolis, Minnesota

Teaching Tips

Before Reading

- Look at the cover of the book. Discuss the picture and the title.
- Ask readers to brainstorm a list of what they already know about cows. What can they expect to see in the book?
- Go on a picture walk, looking through the pictures to discuss vocabulary and make predictions about the text.

During Reading

- Read for purpose. Encourage readers to think about cows and the animal life cycle as they are reading.
- If readers encounter an unknown word, ask them to look at the sounds in the word. Then, ask them to look at the rest of the page. Are there any clues to help them understand?

After Reading

- Encourage readers to pick a buddy and reread the book together.
- Ask readers to name three things cows do between the time they are born and the time they are ready to have babies. Go back and find the pages that tell about these things.
- Ask readers to write or draw something that they learned about cows.

Credits:
Cover, © jeffstrauss/ iStock; 3, © Dmytro Leschenko/ Shutterstock; 5, © emholk/ iStock; 6,7, © Bernilynn/ iStock; 8, © Martin Bergsma/ Shutterstock; 9, © Africa Studio/ Shutterstock; 9, © TeaML/ Shutterstock; 10,11, © mrohana/ iStock; 12, © emholk/ iStock; 14,15, © symbiot/ Shutterstock; 15, © Wichai Prasomsri1/ Shutterstock; 17, © Singh Virender/ Shutterstock; 18, © Clara Bastian/ iStock; 19, © Africa Studio/ Shutterstock; 20, © xpixel/ Shutterstock; 21, © DutchScenery/ iStock; 22, © baona/ iStock; 23, © debibishop/ iStock; 23, © B Brown/ Shutterstock; 23, © adamkaz/ iStock; 23, © Fazwick/ Shutterstock.

Library of Congress Cataloging-in-Publication Data

Names: Boothroyd, Jennifer, 1972- author.
Title: Baby cows / by Jennifer Boothroyd.
Description: Bearcub books. | Minneapolis, Minnesota : Bearport Publishing Company, [2022] | Series: Animal babies | Includes bibliographical references and index.
Identifiers: LCCN 2021026724 (print) | LCCN 2021026725 (ebook) | ISBN 9781636913544 (library binding) | ISBN 9781636913612 (paperback) | ISBN 9781636913681 (ebook)
Subjects: LCSH: Calves--Juvenile literature. | Cows--Juvenile literature.
Classification: LCC SF197.5 .B66 2022 (print) | LCC SF197.5 (ebook) | DDC 636.2/07--dc23
LC record available at https://lccn.loc.gov/2021026724
LC ebook record available at https://lccn.loc.gov/2021026725

For more information, write to Bearport Publishing, 5357 Penn Avenue South, Minneapolis, MN 55419. Printed in the United States of America.

Contents

It's a Baby Cow! 4

The Baby's Body 22

Glossary 23

Index 24

Read More 24

Learn More Online. 24

About the Author 24

It's a Baby Cow!

A baby slides from a mother cow.

Swoosh!

The **calf** is wet.

Its mother licks it dry.

Then, the mother pushes the calf with her nose.

The baby slowly stands on long, skinny legs.

The calf is about the size of a big dog.

It is covered in hair.

The hairy baby takes a few steps to its mother.

The calf is **hungry**.

It drinks milk from its mother's body.

When the calf is full, it is ready to rest.

The baby lies down in the grass.

It takes a nap.

In a few days, the calf is stronger.

The calf and its mother go to live with other cows.

A group of cows is called a **herd**.

The calf runs with the herd.

It kicks and jumps.

The baby grows bigger and bigger.

As it gets older, the calf starts eating grass and **hay**.

After about six months, it stops drinking milk.

It drinks water.

A few months later, the cow is fully grown.

It lives with the herd.

Soon, it will have a baby of its own.

The Baby's Body

Glossary

calf a baby cow

hay grass that is used as food for animals

herd a group of animals that live together

hungry feeling the need for food

Index

eating 19
grass 13, 19
hair 9
hay 19
herd 15–16, 20
milk 10, 19
mother 4, 6, 9–10, 15

Read More

Culliford, Amy. *Cows (Farm Animal Friends).* New York: Crabtree Publishing, 2021.

London, Martha. *Baby Cows (Baby Farm Animals).* Minneapolis: Abdo Publishing, 2021.

Learn More Online

1. Go to **www.factsurfer.com** or scan the QR code below.
2. Enter "**Baby Cows**" into the search box.
3. Click on the cover of this book to see a list of websites.

About the Author

Jennifer Boothroyd's favorite cow breeds are Ankole and Scottish Highland.